# A Brief History of the
# Fakahatchee

**ISLANDS & RIVERS**

**LOGGING THE CYPRESS**

**DEVELOPMENT BY GULF AMERICAN**

**THE FIGHT TO SAVE THIS UNIQUE ECOLOGY**

**Marya Repko**

ECITY • PUBLISHING

**More South Florida books from this publisher:**

*A Brief History of the Everglades City Area*
*The Story of Everglades City; A History for Younger Readers*
*Historia de Everglades City*
*Words on the Wilderness: Place Names in South Florida National Parks*
*Angel of the Swamp; Deaconess Harriet Bedell in the Everglades*
*Frog Poop & other stories*

---

**A Brief History of the Fakahatchee**

Copyright © 2009 text by Marya Repko, All Rights Reserved.

Front cover illustration from a painting by Jim Bob Singletary
Back cover Ghost Orchid sketch from a photograph by Jay Staton Photography

Set in Bookman Old Style, 11/16 pt
Printed and Bound in the U. S. A.

First Edition, First Printing, November 2009

ISBN  978-0-9716006-8-3

ECity • Publishing

P O Box 5033
Everglades City, FL, 34139
telephone (239) 695-2905
ecitypublishing@earthlink.net
www.ecity-publishing.com

# PREFACE

This is a saga about the fight to save a unique natural area in southwest Florida but it is also the history of the pioneers who scratched out a living among our local islands and the loggers who slogged in the great swamp and the developers who almost destroyed it.

If you are a native Floridian, you probably learned at school, or lived through, much of the background about drainage and conservation. However, many residents are new to Florida and do not know the history, as I didn't until I started reading and researching.

My deep gratitude to Captain Franklin Adams who shared his memories, his notes, his photos, and his Mel Finn files with me.

My thanks also to neighbors and friends who told me stories about olden days to make history come alive. Special mention goes to Janet Treadway who has a nostalgic love of this area, to Jim Bob Singletary for his generosity with artwork, and to those members of the Friends of Fakahatchee who contributed recollections and photos.

Finally, I would like to acknowledge those special people who read through drafts and red-penciled errors. I would be glad to hear from readers of any further corrections or suggestions.

Marya Repko

Everglades City

October, 2009

**YOU NEVER KNOW WHAT YOU MIGHT SEE IN THE FAKAHATCHEE STRAND PRESERVE.**
*Clamshell orchid (top left) courtesy of FOF members Jim & Niki Woodard.*
*Ghost Orchid (top right) courtesy of FOF member Jay Staton.*
*Barred Owl courtesy of FOF member Jay Staton.*
*Baby gators at the Boardwalk courtesy of FOF members Caryl & Nelson Tilden.*
*Panther and bear on Janes Drive courtesy of Mike Jerrard.*
*Deer in Dan House Prairie courtesy of FOF members Jim & Niki Woodard.*

# CONTENTS

INTRODUCTION                                    1

HISTORICAL BACKGROUND              3

ISLANDS AND RIVERS                        9

LOGGING THE CYPRESS                    13

LIFE IN A LOGGING TOWN               23

GULF AMERICAN                               29

SAVING THE GREATER GLADES      35

SAVING THE STRAND                        37

BIG CYPRESS BEND                          45

THE PRESERVE AND FRIENDS        47


SOURCES                                          53


TIMELINE                                          58

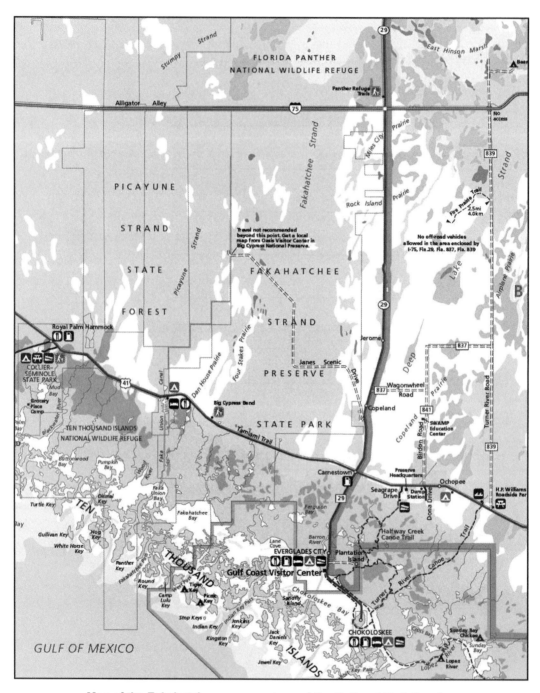

*Map of the Fakahatchee area courtesy of the National Park Service.*

# INTRODUCTION

It has been called the "Fahkahatchee", "Fathahatchee", "Fickahatchee", "Fackeehatchee", Fikahatchee", "Fahkahatchie". The word is generally thought to mean "forked river" in the Miccosukee language. The U. S. Geological Survey in 1927 lists it:[1]

> Fakahatchee; river, Collier County, Fla., emptying into Chokoloskee Bay, 11 miles east of Cape Romano (Not Fah-kah-hatchee, Fahkahnatcheea, Fakanachi, nor Fakanachia).

The name is attached to a slough, a strand, a river, an island, a bay, and a park. They are all in Southwest Florida. The land is often referred to as part of the Big Cypress. The slough (pronounced "slew") is the area of lowest elevation into which surrounding waters from the higher elevations (the strand) flow. Fakahatchee Strand is about 20 miles long and 3 to 5 miles wide:[2]

> Strands are swamps unique to Florida ... [they] follow nearly level depressions over limestone ... Fakahatchee Strand is the largest and it is unrivaled in its many unusual and rare plants and animals.

It is home to cypress, pine, royal palms, orchids and bromeliads and other epiphytes, and to many animals, some endangered. It has been described as:[3]

> ... the heartland of the Big Cypress ... [the Fakahatchee] includes samples of almost every landscape to be found anywhere in the Big Cypress Swamp ... one of the most extraordinary plant communities in North America – a hammock swamp of bald cypress and royal palm ... places in the strand that probably have no equal for their abundance of ghost orchids, swamp lilies, and bird's-nest ferns"

Further south, the river drains into the bay. Fakahatchee Island was once inhabited by farmers and fishermen. The river and slough were known to early Native Americans who traveled north and south in the greater glades:[4]

> A series of canoe routes ... began in the Ten Thousand Islands and extended northward through the Big Cypress probably along the Fakahatchee Swamp route. One branch route led from this

---

[1] *Decisions of the United States Geographic Board, June 1923 – June 1927*, United States Government Printing Office, Washington, 1927, p.12

[2] Larson, *Swamp Song*, pp. 24-26

[3] Carr, *The Everglades*, pp. 48-50

[4] Davis, "The Natural Features of Southern Florida", p.21

swamp to Lake Trafford where a number of mounds are located. Another branch route went up the Okaloacoochee Slough to the Caloosahatchee River, then into Lake Okeechobee ...

In the 150 or more years since this area was explored by white men, its trees have been felled and it has been threatened by development. Fortunately, the strand has recovered and its unique ecology is now preserved as a State Park.

**Ted Smallwood in front of his store in Chokoloskee.**
**The Storter store and homestead on the river in Everglade in 1915.**
*Photos courtesy of the Florida State Archives, Photographic Collection.*

# HISTORICAL BACKGROUND

Florida was established as the 27th State of the Union in 1845 with Tallahassee as its capital.

Settlers and Native Americans had both started moving southward; settlers for a better climate, Indians to escape being sent to reservations in Oklahoma by the Federal government. The Seminole Wars were fought from the early 1800s onwards. By the time the conflicts ended in 1858, U. S. Army forts had been built along both Florida coasts and inland. A few Seminoles and Miccosukees were still camping in the deep glades.

As early as the 1830s, there were thoughts about draining the Everglades:[5]

> Could it be drained by deepening the natural outlets? Would it not open to cultivation immense tracts of rich vegetable soil? Could the waterpower, obtained by draining, be improved to any useful purpose? Would such draining render the country unhealthy?

Dispatches about the southern peninsula had been sent to Washington by Colonel Harney and Lieutenant McLaughlin during the Second Seminole War (1835-1848). In 1848 Thomas Buckingham Smith produced a report to the Senate recommending drainage:[6]

> The Ever Glades are now suitable only for the haunt of noxious vermin or the resort of pestilent reptiles. That statesman whose exertions shall cause the millions of acres they contain, now worse than worthless, to team with the products of agricultural industry ... will merit a high place in public favor ...

In 1850, an Act of Congress was passed giving the State some of the territory on condition that "proceeds of the sale of any of the lands so granted should be applied exclusively to the purposes of reclaiming the swamp and overflowed lands"[7] and the Florida Internal Improvement Fund was formed in early 1851.

The first major drainage project was started by Hamilton Disston in 1881 when he bought 4 million acres (at $0.25 each) in the Kissimmee area but ended with his sudden death in 1896.

---

[5] John Lee Williams, *The Territory of Florida*, quoted in Dovell, "The Everglades Before Reclamation", p.20

[6] Thomas Buckingham Smith, "Report of Buckingham Smith, Esquire, on His Reconnaissance of the Everglades, 1848", quoted in Dovell, "The Everglades Before Reclamation", p.33

[7] quoted in Dovell, "The Everglades Before Reclamation", p.37

Napoleon Bonaparte Broward promised in his 1904 gubernatorial campaign to drain the glades, despite objections from early conservationists like Frank Stoneman of the *Miami Herald*. The digging of the North New River canal and the straightening of the Caloosahatchee River allowed the inaugural coast-to-coast steamship passage from Fort Lauderdale to Fort Myers in April 1912.

The first land boom was on. Extensive advertising offered land south of Lake Okeechobee at $50 per acre ($2.00 down and $2.00 per month). However, Florida land sales soon gained a bad name because drainage had not taken place as fast as promised and many of the lots were still under water much of the time. Where settlements did take place, the hardships of pioneer life and the vagaries of the weather discouraged many from staying in the area.

Fortunately for the Fakahatchee, the planned canals from the Lake to the Gulf were not dredged.

Settlers had begun arriving at southern Florida's coastal fringes after the Civil War. They farmed, fished, hunted, and traded with the Indians, taking produce to market by boat. The only large city was Key West, a major shipping port and seat of Monroe County which stretched as far north as the Caloosahatchee River. Adventurous pioneers carved out homesteads near Fort Myers to the west and around Biscayne Bay on the east. By the 1880s they were cultivating the Ten Thousand Islands and adjacent river banks. Lee County was formed in 1887 with the newly-incorporated City of Fort Myers as its seat.

There were no major roads but the railways were creeping south. Henry Flagler's Florida East Coast Railway was extended to Miami in 1896 and encouraged settlers looking for a warm climate. By the early 1920s, Carl Fisher had created Miami Beach by filling in a mangrove swamp. Land changed hands in the Miami area for huge sums.

Henry Plant's Atlantic Coast Line (ACL) reached Tampa in 1885 and Fort Myers in 1904. In 1921 it went as far as Immokalee, a ranching and truck-farming town.

Further afield, the Storter and Smallwood founding families in Everglade and Chokoloskee had well-established trading posts to deal with the locals as well as Native Americans. Both men learned some of the Indian language and were respected by the natives. Agricultural products (fruits, vegetables, sugar cane syrup) were shipped out to Key West or Fort Myers regularly. Alligator hides, raccoon skins and salted fish brought cash to the frontier when taken to market. The settlements were civilized but self-sufficient.

Into this remote rural environment at the beginning of the roaring 1920s came Barron Gift Collier, a streetcar-advertising millionaire, with hope and determination. He bought up hundreds of thousands of acres of raw land in southwest Florida. His first purchase in the wilderness was the Deep Lake citrus farm started in 1913 by streetcar colleague John Roach of Chicago and Fort Myers business leader Walter Langford. Besides the lush crop, the plantation had a primitive rail line to the navigable river in the coastal village of Everglade.

Collier was not the only entrepreneur with grandiose plans for the area. Miami tax assessor J. F. Jaudon platted a city near Lostman's River on a property owned by eccentric French botanist Jean Chevalier. With Jaudon's encouragement, the authorities in Tampa and Miami had begun a road between their cities, a cross-Florida overland link which would save the long boat trip around Florida Bay or via Lake Okeechobee and the canals.

Construction of the Tamiami Trail began in 1915 at both ends with Jaudon routing the eastern section through his lands around Pinecrest, now in the Big Cypress National Preserve. Lee County on the west coast progressed to a point near Naples and ran out of money.

In 1923, Collier offered to finance the completion of the Trail through swamp and forest if a county were created for him encompassing the great expanse of land he had accumulated. He made the town of Everglade his county seat and construction headquarters and hired former U. S. Navy engineer David Graham Copeland as his manager. Collier renamed "Everglade" by adding an "s" and used family names for other geographic locations (eg, Barron River after himself, Carnestown after his wife, Miles City for one of his sons).

During the five years from 1923 to 1928 that it took to build roads and city, one of the raw materials needed was lumber. Collier's people set up sawmills, first in DuPont across the river from Everglades town center and then at the junction of the Deep Lake rail track and SR-29, about 2 miles north of the Trail (now US-41). By 1927 the logging road went 11 miles into the woods to a stand of pine. Logs were dragged out, cut for bridges and buildings, and shipped via rail.

In 1928, the Trail was completed as well as the Immokalee Road (now SR-29) with a full-gauge rail track parallel to it. Atlantic Coast Line (ACL) trains went to the southern end of the line at the Everglades depot (now the Everglades Seafood Depot Restaurant).

The area was ripe for development. Tomato farms were begun on the Trail at Ochopee by James Gaunt and on the ACL at Copeland by the Janes brothers and Alfred Webb. Little towns sprung up around them. More logging operations were set up in the Big Cypress at Pinecrest and near Ochopee.

It was the era of paternalistic society, a throwback to feudalism with the best intentions. Workers were housed, entertainment provided, favors granted, emergencies dealt with, but all the assets were owned by the company and personal finances were restricted by the payment of wages in "scrip" or "babbit" which could only be spent in the company stores.

The 1926 and 1928 hurricanes plus the 1929 economic depression ended the second land boom.

However, World War II created a need for lumber. Cypress was used in the construction of PT boats and on the decks of aircraft carriers. Pine was sent abroad to build military bases.

And, after the war, many of the soldiers, sailors, and airmen who had trained in Florida's pleasant climate decided to return. It was time to start developing again.

**Rob Storter (1894-1987) remembers carrying supplies up the Fakahatchee River to the Tamiami Trail ("this wonderful road") when it was being built in the 1920s.**
*Sketch from the Storter Collection, Courtesy of the Collier County Museum, Naples, FL.*

**The Atlantic Coast Line (ACL) Rail Road depot in Everglades City in the 1930s.**
*Photo courtesy of the Florida State Archives, Photographic Collection.*

Rob Storter (1894-1987) remembers the Fakahatchee where John Daniels raised a large family around 1916 and laments that it has become all overgrown with bushes and trees. *Sketch from the Storter Collection, Courtesy of the Collier County Museum, Naples, FL.*

The Woods family fishing camp built in an old ice house in Fakahatchee Bay in the 1950s and the ruins after it caught on fire in 1964. *Photos courtesy of Don Woods.*

# ISLANDS AND RIVERS

Charles Torrey Simpson wrote in 1920:[8]

> "The Ten Thousand Islands is a region of mystery and loneliness; gloomy, monotonous, weird and strange, yet possessing a decided fascination,"

However, to some, it was home. Locals talk about parents or grandparents who grew up on the islands. They also have stories about fishing in the mangrove maze or venturing up the rivers.

Many of the islands had been occupied when the Spanish arrived in the 1500s by early Native Americans, probably the Calusa who left artifacts like the famous cat on Marco. Various islands still have shell mounds, some of which contain human bones. A shell and soil mound was also reported about 4 miles up the Fakahatchee River.

White settlers came in the 1880s, moved around the area, and left or died or sold out. A few of the family names are still prominent on the mainland: Daniels, Demere, Hamilton, Smith, Thompson.

During a survey of Chokoloskee Bay and its surroundings in 1883, early Everglades settler William Smith Allen wrote to the Deputy Surveyor in Key West with names of all the local families some of whom (Phineas Myers, John Ferguson, and David Roberts)[9] can be placed on the islands.

The right side of the Fakahatchee River was farmed from 1890 to 1900 with sweet potatoes and sugar cane. The owner, a Swede named Charles Echolm, also cut buttonwood and made charcoal, a lucrative commodity in Key West where it was used for cooking. He sold out to John Henry Daniels and the homestead was referred to as "the old Daniels' place".[10] It is now known locally as "Daniels' Point".

Fakahatchee Island was occupied by J. S. Hart, H. B. Smith, David Roberts, and others. The shell mound at the north end was home to James Demere from 1890 until 1895 when his wife died in childbirth and

---

[8] Simpson, *In Lower Florida Wilds*, p.74

[9] Knetsch, Joe, "Surveying Chokoloskee's Wilderness World", *South Florida History Magazine, Winter 1993*, HMSF, Miami, FL, pp. 11-14

[10] Copeland, D. Graham, *Data Relative to Florida*, Everglades, FL, 1947, typescript in the Florida State Library, p.1112

he left. In 1888 Jim Yeoman lived on the island and took produce for himself and others in his sailboat to Marco. He and one of his neighbors, Adrian Chamberlain, argued so much that when Chamberlain was shot in 1890, Yeoman fled to the Bahamas accompanied by his brother and a young C. S. (Ted) Smallwood who "went with them to see the country."[11] Yeoman was arrested ten years later by the newly-elected Sheriff Tippins but acquitted of the killing. He lived on the Shell Mound until he sold out to Barron Collier in 1922. Another resident was John Henry Thompson who had captained Edgar Watson's boat before moving around the islands.

There were enough children on Fakahatchee Island for Lee County to grant a school in 1903. The building was destroyed by a tornado in 1909 and rebuilt. When Collier County was formed in 1923, the land was turned over to the County. One of the teachers was George Storter's daughter Frankie (Frances) who was the first white child born in Everglade. Another teacher is quoted: [12]

> ... most of the families were fishermen. Many were rough in type and behavior but the school children were well behaved and interested.

Nearby Russell Island was briefly home to David Roberts and then to Phineas B. Myers, when it was called "Phin's Island". J. W. Russell moved there from Clearwater with his 6 sons and 2 daughters in 1893 and sold half the island to a family named Gaston who had a chicken farm. Rob Storter, born in Everglade village in 1894, remembers being taken as a small boy to Russell Island where the Gastons on the west side sold eggs at 30¢ a dozen. In 1899 Russell moved to Naples and then to Oregon and in 1904 the island was bought by Walter Langford of Fort Myers who had it surveyed.

The most famous resident of the islands was probably Juan Gomez who lived on Panther Key. He claimed to have fought with Napoleon's army in 1805 and to have escaped from pirates, possibly Gaspar's crew. By the 1890's he was well-known by locals and received regular supplies from Marco Island. He died in 1900, when he was reputedly age 122.

---

[11] quoted in Tebeau, Charlton W., *The Story of Chokoloskee Bay Country*, Florida Flair Books, Miami, FL, 1976, p.72

[12] Mrs. Leola Thomas Leifeste quoted in Stone, Donald O., and Beth W. Carter, *The First 100 Years; Lee Country Public Schools, 1887-1987*, Lee County School Board, Fort Myers, FL, n/d, p.69

An example of life in 1925 is given by Rob Storter when he describes fishing at Dismal Key, just up the coast:[13]

> It was closed season on mullet but the law was not enforced and Sheriff Manard [Maynard] was on our side. We had Mr. McKinney get us two hundred sacks of coarse fish salt (160-pound bags). ... Fish were plentiful ... I have never seen such a bunch of mullet ... every net was as full as it could hold. We estimated ten thousand head ... in a few minutes all our nets were sunk down with mullet ... We worked all that day, all night, and all the next day ... In ten days we put up one hundred barrels of salt mullet. We hired Riggs Fish Company to haul them to Key West. We got four and a half cents a pound for the mullet and ten cents for the roe.

Totch Brown recalls fishing in 1934 up the Fakaunie River (now the Faka Union Canal):[14]

> ... covered in places with overhanging limbs entangled together, so it was like paddling up a tunnel ... after a couple of hours we came to the first bay ... schools of mullet jumping ... having a party.

Don Woods remembers the islands when he was taken there as a young boy by his family from Miami for fishing vacations. His father and uncle bought an abandoned fish house on stilts in Fakahatchee Bay from the Riggs Fish Company in 1950. It had been an icehouse to store the catch until it could be taken to the ACL train in Everglades. The camp which they nicknamed the "Fakahatchee Yacht Club"[15] provided them much pleasure until they discovered on Labor Day Weekend, 1964, that it had been struck by lightning and burned down so that only the pilings were left.

Another fishing visitor, in the late 1940s and early 1950s, remembers as a child that "we had to go there when the tides were right or we would run aground. And if you didn't know where you were going, you would get lost because all the mangroves looked alike" and that the Daniels boy "was always barefooted on that crushed shell island".[16]

There are two interesting connections between the islands and the strand.

The Ferguson River was called Lane River and a Lane Cove is still shown on maps. The shell mound at the mouth of the river was farmed for fruit

---

[13] Storter, *Crackers in the Glade*, p.86

[14] Brown, *Totch*, p.91

[15] Wood, Donald, "The Ruins; Reflections on an Everglades Family Fishing Camp", *Florida Sportsman, December 2005*, pp. 44-50

[16] email correspondence with the author

by John Ferguson from 1881 until he sold out to Phineas B. Myers in 1886. The property then passed to John Henry Daniels who sold to a man named Layne who never lived there. Layne sold to Gandees in 1900. After that, there is a reference to a Mrs. Thompson who lived at "the old Layne Place".[17] The coincidence is that the *Liparis elata* and *Cranichis muscos* orchids were discovered in 1903 in the Fakahatchee Strand by James E. Layne who died shortly thereafter.[18] Local residents can not explain why it is called Lane Cove.

The other coincidence is that the grandson of Phineas B. Myers became a game warden in the Fakahatchee Strand. Myer's daughter Mary Virginia married Henry Smith, a carpenter, and they lived on Russell Island for a while and then moved to the mainland. As an adult in the Depression and afterwards, their son Hilburn killed alligators to sell their hides for a living and finally took a job with Remuda Ranch catching poachers. The Smith family is still active in the Everglades area but in more traditional occupations.

The completion of Tamiami Trail in 1928 shifted focus from the water to the land. The commercial fishermen who were left found the local waters closed to them after the National Park was formed in 1947. Writing in 1957, historian Charlton Tebeau reported that there were still a few people on the Fakahatchee Island and that Clifford Daniels was living in the old schoolhouse. By the 1980s, a scattering of hermits remained on the islands and only sports fishermen were allowed to harvest the waters.

Russell Island is now within the Everglades National Park boundary and Fakahatchee Island belongs to the State. The Fakahatchee River and East River are part of the Fakahatchee Strand Preserve.

---

[17] Storter, *Crackers in the Glade*, p.56

[18] Correll, Donovan Stewart, *Native Orchids of North America*, Chronica Botanica, Waltham, MA, 1950, p.273

# LOGGING THE CYPRESS

The history of logging companies in Florida is complicated, to say the least. Personnel and organizations seem to be inter-twined. It mostly started in the Panhandle where pine was cut and turpentine produced near the naval town of Pensacola. As pine forests were diminished, the loggers moved southward. Hardwoods like cypress became valuable to out-of-state concerns who were ready to brave the swamps.

There were four companies who were eventually involved, some indirectly, with the logging operation in Fakahatchee. The complication arises in the chain of cooperative arrangements and takeovers which resulted in the Lee Tidewater Cypress Company:

Brooks-Scanlon was founded 1896 in Minneapolis and established in the north and west of the United States. In 1917 they bought Carpenter-O'Brien and operated the mill at Eastport until 1929 when they built a new mill in a town they called Foley in honor of their manager.

Burton-Swartz moved from Louisiana to Florida in 1914 and built a sawmill in Perry so that they could cut the cypress which was on land logged for pine by Carpenter-O'Brien. The companies established a joint logging camp called "Carbur" from which cypress went to the mill in Perry and pine went to the Eastport mill.

Carpenter-O'Brien started a pine mill in Eastport in 1913 and held 48% of Burton-Swartz after their joint venture was agreed. In 1917 Brooks-Scanlon bought out Carpenter-O'Brien and, thus, owned 48% of Burton-Swartz.

J. C. Turner Cypress Lumber Company was founded by John Charles Turner in 1895 with a distribution yard in New York on the Hudson River. He transported cypress from Louisiana and Florida. One of his suppliers was Burton-Swartz. In 1910 J. C. Turner built a cypress mill in Centralia, Florida.

In 1913, J. C. Turner and Captain W. L. Burton bought 150,000 acres of virgin cypress in the Everglades from the Florida Cypress Company of Michigan who had bought the land in 1907 from men named

Butterworth and Kenney. Burton-Swartz owned 60% and J. C. Turner, 40%. In 1924 the Lee Cypress Company was formed as a holding company.

Burton-Swartz stopped logging in 1943. The mill in Perry and the land holdings were taken over by Turner Lumber under the name Lee Cypress Company which was changed in 1947 to Lee Tidewater Cypress Company. By this time, Burton, Swartz, and Turner had all died. J. Arthur Currey, who had started working for Turner at age 14, was president of the new company which incorporated the remnants of the four founding businesses.

Most of the easily-accessible cypress had been logged in Florida by the early 1940s when Lee Cypress did a trial cut of 2 acres in the Fakahatchee strand near the town of Copeland. That trial filled 4 railroad cars with logs which produced 28,000 board feet of lumber at the mill in Perry. Randolph Swain, later the logging boss, remembers "It was so pecky that we eased outside of what they had measured for us to cut and took some other good trees."[19]

A tree is described as "pecky" when it has wormy grooves caused by a fungus. The disease dies when the tree is cut. The wood could not be sold and was thrown away or used for local buildings. It is now considered valuable.

Arthur Currey agreed with the Atlantic Coast Line Railroad (ACL) that Lee Cypress would ship full trains of 40 cars from Copeland to Perry and that ACL could carry the finished lumber away from Perry. ACL also leased rails to the lumber company for their tracks in the forest.

The logging operation involved teams of specialists. A "cruiser" picked out trees to be cut. A ring was chopped around the trunk, a process called "girdling", so that the tree died and most of its water content drained away. A path was hacked out through the undergrowth, usually by Miccosukee Indians, and then a roadbed was built up by digging a "borrow canal" next to it. The "steel gang" would lay track, on the spur lines about 1600 feet apart. Finally, the sawyers were taken on the logging train to the girdled trees where they cut them down, trimmed

---

[19] Swain, *Memories of Randolph Swain*, p.30

them, and sawed them into lengths that would fit in the railroad cars ("gondalas").

A *National Geographic* article in 1948 describes the scene:[20]

> ... in the almost impenetrable Fakahatchee Slough, a long strip of virgin cypress is the largest remaining single stand in the United States ... A high line run from a skidder was snaking fat trees out of jungle so thick we could see only a few yards into it ... We watched a team of fallers topple a big cypress with a double-handled saw. With a sound like close thunder the soaring giant crashed through lower growth to smite the ground with a booming thud. "That one is between 500 and 750 years old," stated Terrill [logging superintendent]. "Not a very old one. It's surprising how sound and healthy they are, after standing up to their knees in water all their lives – and without their rubbers!"

Journalist Nixon Smiley wrote about his visit in 1953:[21]

> The main line has reached a point about twenty-six miles from the Copeland headquarters, and there are many branch lines. When the cutting has been finished along one of these branch lines, the tracks and cross ties are pulled up and laid down in a new area ... When you see how this timber is gotten out of the wet swamps, it makes you wonder how such an operation can be run at a profit, even with tidewater cypress selling for more than $200 a thousand feet. More than 200 persons, from rail-layers to train engineers, are employed on the job.

The following year, "Loggers of the Unknown Swamp" by Jeanne Van Holmes appeared in *The Saturday Evening Post*":[22]

> Many of these big old cypress trees are still with us today because of the trouble men have getting ten-ton logs out of the swamp. In Big Cypress the loggers use an overhead cableway skidder. The clanking, roaring fifty-ton skidder heaves the logs out of the water, thirty feet up into the air to an 800-foot heavy steel cable suspended between the skidder's tower and a back spar tree. Then, at 500 feet per minute, it yanks the swinging logs in to the track, crashing them through the standing trees on the way. After thudding their load onto the log pile, the tongs race, open and jumping, back down the cable into the swamp. Here hookers are prowling for other logs to skid out – either sawed cypress or "chocktaws", fallen trees which may be sound or may be full of cottonmouth moccasins.

The skidders burned diesel except for one which had a steam engine and was preferred by Charley Singletary, often called the "Mayor" because he could do everything. The trains used coal for fuel. The engines pulling gondalas stacked with logs went only 5 mph until the track was improved and ties were used to hold the rails together; then they could amble along at 15 mph to the ACL siding.

---

[20] Brown, Andrew H., "Haunting Heart of the Everglades", *National Geographic Magazine, February, 1948*, p.152, p. 169

[21] Smiley, Nixon, "Logging the Last Giants", *The Miami Herald, 1953*, quoted in Kendrick & Walsh; *A History of Florida Forests*, p.271

[22] Holmes, Jeanne Van, "Loggers of the Unknown Swamp", *Saturday Evening Post, March 29, 1954*, pp. 32-33, 102-105

The work trains carrying the men went faster, 25 to 35 mph. However, it could still be a long journey, especially the 57 miles to Corkscrew, a cypress strand north of the Fakahatchee. There was ice on the train for cold drinks and, to while away the hours, they played cards and sang songs and told stories. The train left each morning at 6:00 a.m. and started the return trip from the woods at 4:00 p.m. so loggers put in much shorter days actually "on the job" than those working nearby.

Willie Perry, a sawyer, said, "We'd clean 'round the tree and saw it down ... That's cypress timber. It was pretty hard, but we was used to it. You know, we'd try to beat another fellow cutting."[23] His wife Anna Mae commented, "The work was dangerous. He worked in water up to his waist just about every day. When he came home, he'd look like a wet chicken. But they didn't seem to get sick and hurt like they do today. There wasn't too many accidents."[24]

Logging in Corkscrew was more difficult because it was very swampy. Cypress was also cut to the west but the timber was thinner and had to be combined with the larger logs for the shipments to the sawmill.

Various visitors rode the logging trains including Jack Holmes, a photographer from Miami whose wife Jeanne wrote the *Saturday Evening Post* article in 1954. They were among a number of campaigners, headed by National Audubon Society president John H. Baker, who formed the Corkscrew Cypress Rookery Association which was "established for the acquisition and preservation of the greatest remaining bald cypress swamp and its associated plant and animal life".[25] The rookeries of concern housed thousands of rare wood storks and other birds which had been protected by Audubon wardens as far back as 1912, in the era after plume hunting was made illegal but poachers were still active.

The Association negotiated with J. Arthur Currey of Lee Tidewater Cypress and with Norman Herren of Collier Enterprises. Interested organizations raised $170,000 to purchase 2240 acres from Lee Tidewater. Another 3,200 acres was rented from Collier until $25,000

---

[23] quoted in Stone, *We Also Came*, p.227

[24] quoted in Peterman, *African Americans and the Sawmills of Big Cypress*, p.14

[25] Buckheister, Carl W., "The Acquisition and Development of the Corkscrew Swamp·Sanctuary, 1952-1967", www.corkscrew.audubon.org.

could be paid for the standing timber. Currey's name is remembered in the J. Arthur Currey Forest, an additional 640 acres which his company donated. Over the years, a boardwalk and other amenities for visitors were introduced. The Audubon Corkscrew Sanctuary was dedicated in 1965 as a National Historic Landmark and in 2009 it was added to the list of Wetlands of International Importance.

The sale of Corkscrew brought logging almost to an end. There was still a bit of thinner cypress to the west and then a massive clean-up in the main part of the Fakahatchee. Before the tracks were taken up, they were used by the C. J. Jones Lumber Company to harvest the pine near Corkscrew. Jones had a sawmill in Jerome, a few miles north of Copeland on SR-29, and had been cutting pine since 1940 in the Big Cypress to the east.

Lee Tidewater Cypress had other interests in southwest Florida such as logging for the Babcock Company near LaBelle. They even tried drilling for oil but without success. The J. C. Turner Company's property in Immokalee was farmed for citrus and cattle. Before moving from Copeland, they experimented with rock mining, renting a crusher and a drill for dynamite, but soon sold out to Everglades City businessman Paul Cook.

The locomotives were offered for sale around the area in the early 1960s. Before that, in the winter of 1957-58, Budd Schulberg borrowed Locomotive No. 4 to chug into the Depot in Everglades City for his film "Wind Across the Everglades" which starred Burl Ives, Gypsy Rose Lee, and a young Christopher Plummer.

The locomotives were bought in 1962 by F. Nelson Blount who owned "Steamtown" in Vermont. He died in a plane crash in 1967 and his collection was dispersed. However, it is not clear that the engines were moved because in 1970 some of them went from a siding in Copeland, where they had gathered rust for years, to Monee, Illinois, for the steam railway that John Thompson planned to operate in his winery.

Locomotive No. 4 was moved from there to the Hardin Southern Railroad in Kentucky in 1998 and then in 2009 to its present home at the

Wanamaker, Kempton & Southern Railroad in Kempton, Pennsylvania, where it is being restored.

Locomotive No. 2 found its way in 1988 from Thompson's winery to the Collier County Museum in Naples where it can still be seen.

Locomotive No. 1, which probably never left Perry, went from Blount's estate to the other "Steamtown" in Scranton, Pennsylvania, a National Historic Site operated by the National Park Service.

Other locomotives are reported to be at the Illinois Railway Museum (No. 18), at Kettle Moraine Railway in Wisconsin (No. 16), and in Columbia, South America, (No. 3).

One local resident remembers that Ms. Neal, the biology teacher at Everglades school, took her class out to the Fakahatchee where they rode the train into the woods to see the orchids and other plants.

Pete Ray, a retired electronics engineer and lawyer with a deep interest in orchids, described his adventure amongst the loggers in 1947 when he was a youngster:[26]

It was a simpler time ... A couple of teen-age kids could walk into Tidewater's office and ask if it would be all right if they rode back into the swamps with the timber crew next week. Without a moment's hesitation, the answer came back: "Sure, kids. Be here at 6:00 and bring your own lunch".

We arrived at Copeland to find the crew busy getting everything ready for the day's work. Huge two-man crosscut saws were loaded on the rail cars (there were no power chainsaws then). The locomotive was fired up and the coal supply was loaded. The crew was friendly, mostly black men, some as old as sixty-five, but tough as nails. As first light tinted the sky, we all boarded one of the flatcars, and the train slowly chugged off into the vast cypress swamp. ...We were showered with sparks and ash from the locomotive, but the crew wasn't complaining, and neither were we.

Several miles into the swamp, we arrived at the area currently being cut. The logging crew moved out to the uncut trees, and my buddy and I went to an area where we would be clear of falling trees. Wading in up to two feet of water, we picked our way carefully to avoid the many cottonmouth moccasins. ... Orchids and bromeliads were everywhere. This was (and still is) the prime habitat for the ghost orchid. We searched for specimens growing on smaller branches that could be cut off, since removing the plants from their host without harming them was almost impossible

In a couple of hours, my buddy and I had each gathered a burlap bag of orchid plants, and the rest of the morning was spent watching the timber operations. Since the cutting of these giants was done with handsaws, only a few of them were down before lunchtime. They fell with a

---

[26] Peter C. Ray, "Remembering the Fak", *The Ghost Writer, 10th Anniversary Newsletter, March 2008,* Friends of Fakahatchee, pp. 4-5. See www.friendsoffakahatchee.org.

mighty crash, and then were dragged by the crane to the rail line, crushing everything in their path. It was not a pretty sight. Orchids and bromeliads on the cut trees were wasted, but the stumps were cut about three feet high, and many plants remained on the stumps.

We joined the loggers to eat lunch, and they carried on their conversations just as if we weren't there, giving us a fascinating look at life in a tiny, isolated company town. Nothing was off limits, and stories were told that can't be recounted here. By and large, they seemed happy with their lot – no expectations, no disappointments. Southwest Florida was a frontier as wild as the wild West.

After lunch, we went for a long hike, trying to get away from the noise of the logging operation where we might see some animal life. We saw a cabbage palm that had had its heart torn out by a hungry bear, but the bear was not to be seen. We saw an alligator, small enough not to be a threat. Alligators were rarer then than they are now, having been hunted near extinction for their meat and skin.

The ride back to camp was slow. The little engine barely could, with its load of giant cypress logs, and the shower of ash was heavier than before. The sun was low when we pulled into the camp. We said our goodbyes and thanks, and headed back to Miami in the gathering darkness.

Fahkahatchee Strand is now a State Preserve. A few of the ancient giants remain, and the re-growth is now almost 50 years old. ... It's an area well worth visiting. If you don't mind wet feet, you can see quite a few of the native orchids – with luck, a ghost orchid. Of course, gathering them is now forbidden.

**Pete Ray (right) and friend Mike Knowles during their trip in the Fakahatchee.**
*Photo courtesy of Pete Ray.*

Sawyer Rufus Beebe sharpens his saw with a file.
Girdler Jimmy O'Connor wades to the next tree. Note the ring around the tree behind him.
*Photso courtesy of the Florida State Archives, Photographic Collection.*

Logs were loaded onto a flat car after giant tongs were attached to them.
The tongs were fabricated in the machine shop in Lee Cypress village.
*Photos courtesy of the Florida State Archives, Photographic Collection.*

**Trains took 40 cars of logs twice a week from the Fakahatchee to the mill in Perry.**
*Photo courtesy of the Florida State Archives, Photographic Collection.*
**Inset shows Copeland mainline station with water tower for locomotives.**
*Photo courtesy of FOF member Franklin Adams.*

**Number 2 engine ("Deuce") is now at the Collier County Museum in Naples, seen above with locomotive driver Cecil Oglesby's son Parker and granddaughter Savannah.**
*Photos courtesy of Rudy Oglesby and the Florida State Archives, Photographic Collection.*

Loggers played cards on the long train ride to work.
On the weekends, the blacks relaxed at the "juke" in Lee Cypress.
*Photos courtesy of Clayton Swain, son of the logging boss.*

The Janes Market and Restaurant in Copeland in 2001 after they were closed.
Janes & Company was owned by J. B. Janes and A. B. Webb whose grandson Jim Webb
has a collection of Janes coins, two of which are shown above. *Photos by the author.*

# LIFE IN A LOGGING TOWN

By the early 1940s, the town of Copeland was a thriving tomato-farming center. There were homes for the workers, a packing house, the Janes general store with Post Office, and the Janes restaurant. The currency was "babbit", metal coins stamped with a "J", which could only be used in the company store.

A little train station served Copeland. The ACL took boxes of tomatoes on its way northward to Immokalee and Haines City. Some of the Everglades youngsters enjoyed the adventure of riding the train to Copeland where they were collected by an obliging parent or friend and driven back to the city.

Local residents still distinguish between "Copeland" and the village of "Lee Cypress" which was built by the logging company.

Randolph Swain, who became logging superintendent in 1950, recalled it was "a smooth running operation".[27] He was preceded as the boss by Rich Terrell who was killed in a fight and Roy Baptist who retired with lung cancer.

The work day started with a blast of a whistle "like a community alarm clock"[28] to wake people up for the work train that pulled out at 6:00 a.m. There were other blasts at noon and in the evening a few minutes before the train came back into the camp. An old hunter said that he followed the sound if he were lost in the woods.

Frances Hodge, whose husband was a "steel man" laying tracks, found a job cooking in the white dining hall. Provisions were brought by truck from Miami except for the meat which was bought in the Janes market in Copeland. Before she started work each morning, she prepared a lunch pail for her husband. He was paid $40 a week of which $3 went for rent.

Anna Mae Perry picked tomatoes, drove the black school bus, and worked in the school lunch room. She was also a midwife and was

---

[27] Swain, *Memories of Randolph Swain*, p.42

[28] Frances Hodge quoted in Peterman, *African Americans and the Sawmills of Big Cypress*, p.11

known throughout the county as "Mother Perry". She delivered over 500 black and white babies and had an annual birthday party for them each June until her passing in October 2008 at age 98.

David Graham Copeland, manager of the Collier interests, wrote in an update in 1945 for men and women serving during the war:[29]

> The Lee Cypress Company is making rapid strides in the Big Cypress and now is shipping logs to the mill at Perry, Florida, at the rate of about nine trainloads – each with more than forty cars – monthly. Their camp near Copeland is a beehive of activity and gives employment to more than 250 men. The population of the camp is now about 750 persons.

In the mid-1950s, there were about 30 houses for white and about 50 for blacks. The Indians had their own camp nearby. A power plant with 3 generators served the area and a crew of 3 maintenance men took care of the houses, waterworks, office, and two churches.

There were no schools and the children went by bus to either the white school in Everglades or the black school in DuPont. Religious services were held in the black church by Baptist, Methodist, and Holiness preachers on rotating Sundays. The white church was a Baptist Mission. There was also a Pentecostal church on SR-29.

Friday night was a time to relax. As families waited to be paid, Monroe Graham sold boiled peanuts and cold drinks. The whites would go across SR-29 to Janes Restaurant. The blacks had a juke in Lee Cypress and would go to a hatch at the back of Janes if they wanted to buy drink. The blacks also had a movie theater but the whites went by bus to see films at the community clubhouse in Everglades.

Janet Treadway, who lived in Lee Cypress during the mid-1950s, recalls:[30]

> There was also a play area where we shot baskets in an old tomato basket on a post, played baseball, etc. Some kind man would build a fire in a drum for us kids on cold days while we waited for our bus to go to Everglades to go to school. When the rain caused flooding, men made wood walkways so we could get around in the camp. Some of us talk about our years there and how poor we were and did not even know it, and what a wonderful time we had together.

---

[29] Copeland, David Graham, letter dated 3/10/1945, reproduced as *Caring Colliers* by WinCar Hardware, Everglades City, FL, 2004, p.7

[30] email correspondence with the author

I remember that they only dug 12 feet down to get fresh water. It was so rusty that if you let a glass of water set, rust would settle in the bottom. That's when I learned to enjoy ice tea. My mother boiled all the water and when she made ice tea you could not taste the rust.

An interesting thing I remember about the camp was the rolling stores ... the fruit and vegetable truck, the clothing van, and a furniture truck from Babcock. ... I can still see in my mind's eye the ladies hurrying out to these rolling stores. Of course, a lot of stuff was purchased out of catalogs also.

She also remembers a bear being cut up for meat after it was shot, watching TV at the home of the Copeland Post Master with bunches of other kids in the neighborhood (there was only one station, from Miami), and how everyone helped each other.

Cecil Oglesby, Jr., whose father came from Perry to drive one of the trains, recalls that "we were all one big group, black and white together."[31] Although most people moved back to Northern Florida after logging stopped, some are still in the area. Cecil is now a local fishing guide.

After integration, the black church closed and was given to Ms. Frances as the oldest living member. She wanted the little building to be restored for the community but passed away 2 days before her 101st birthday in 2007. The Janes store and Post Office complex were sold to the National Park Service to be addition lands for Big Cypress National Preserve and were torn down in 2002.

Winford Janes, one of the three brothers involved in the tomato farm, became a Collier County Commissioner and an active resident in the community. After his death in 1962, the old mainline logging tram, which by that time was a County road called locally "the Copeland Grade", was named Janes Memorial Scenic Drive.

The town was bought from the J. C. Turner Company in 1975 by Douglas McGoon who worked for the company. His intention was to farm tomatoes. He let residents buy the lots they were living on and donated land near the Baptist Mission for the community.

---

[31] quoted in Stone, *We Also Came*, p.227

The "Red Barn" was the machine shop and electricity generating plant for Lee Cypress. It was abandoned after logging stopped and bought in 1985 by a retired professor to be restored. It burned down in late 1990. The water tower was demolished in early 1991.
*Picture from a painting by Jim Bob Singletary.*

Ms Frances Hodge celebrated her 100th birthday on August 22, 2006. She and her husband
worked for the Lee Tidewater company. The Bula Baptist Mission was given to her.
*Photos by the author.*

Norman Herren worked for the Collier companies and was also on the State Forestry Board.
"Mother" Anna Mae Perry delivered hundreds of babies and was the wife of a sawyer.
*Photo by the author at the Museum of the Everglades on December 8, 2001.*

Aerial photo taken in 1981 of Remuda Ranch (now called Port of the Islands).
The Faka Union Canal runs south towards Fakahatchee Bay at top of picture.
*Photo courtesy of Florida State Archives, Photographic Collection.*

# GULF AMERICAN

In 1957 the Rosen brothers from Baltimore bought 1,724 acres of mangrove swamp west of Fort Myers on the Caloosahatchee River. They dredged canals, filled housing lots, and built roads. The new sub-division was named Cape Coral and a high-pressure sales campaign began all over the country and even in Europe. They advertised "a community where a person did not have to be a millionaire in order to live like one".[32]

Leonard and Jack Rosen had learnt about television advertising when they made their first fortune selling shampoo. With more at stake, their Gulf American Corporation offered free meals, trips to Florida, and even Green Stamps to potential customers. Best of all, land was sold on an installment plan: $120 down and $20 per month.

Some purchasers were not happy when they discovered their lots had no utilities and that no infrastructure existed in what was supposed to be a new town. There was a country club but no schools or stores. Vacant lots, untended canals, and buckling roads were eyesores. The land, built up from dredged material, did not support lush gardens and the whole layout was on a boring grid.

Gulf American's next venture was to accumulate a large tract in Collier County. In 1960 the company bought 26,000 acres, followed in 1962 by 7,500 acres of "cut-over cypress" southwest of Corkscrew and 28,000 acres from J. C. Turner. To round out the purchase, they bought 44,600 acres from the Collier corporation, giving the Rosen brothers a blank slate of 175 square miles.

The whole area was called Golden Gate Estates. A small city named Golden Gate was built east of Naples and sold well. Another city, Golden Gate North, was started near Immokalee.

The rest of the territory was parceled out in large lots of 5 acres each. The pitch was the investment potential in raw land. "Buy by the acre, sell

---

[32] quoted in Dodrill, *Selling the Dream*, p.82

by the lot".[33] People bought but very few tried to build and live in the unserviced area.

The Estates stretched from north of what is now I-75 to US-41 at the south. The dredges and road-building tore up virgin forest and flattened the landscape. The outlet for all the inconvenient water was a widened and deepened Fakaunie River, renamed the Faka Union Canal, which spilled torrents into the Ten Thousand Islands. The area, barren and mostly uninhabited, a grid of canals and roads, became known as "the blocks" or "south blocks". The remote empty streets were ideal landing strips for drug runners' airplanes or drag strips for young car racers and older ATV drivers.

Following their policy to acquire property neighboring their other developments, in 1966 Gulf American bought 68,000 acres, some of it cut-over timber land in the Fakahatchee from the J. C. Turner company, and named the parcel Remuda Ranch Grants (a "remuda" is a stable of spare saddle horses). Two hotels, one on either side of the Tamiami Trail, were built. There was a skeet shooting range, stable of horses, marina, and dockage but no improvements to the land itself. Purchasers were expected to set up camp on their lots (1.25 acres cost $1,250), if they could find them, and then enjoy the amenities of the Spanish-style hotels.

John Rothchild describes Remuda Ranch as:[34]

> an Alhambra rising out of the wetlands on both sides of the highway ... centerpiece for an under-water subdivision ... a community of absentee property holders.

Gulf American's sales practices came to the attention of the Florida Installment Land Sales Board (FILSB) after complaints that lots had been switched and that too much pressure to sign contracts was exerted on customers. Frustrated by Florida state politics, Gulf American sold out in 1969 to a Philadelphia finance firm General Acceptance Corporation who formed a subsidiary named (confusingly) GAC Properties and tried to satisfy their customers. Sales at Remuda Ranch stopped and owners were offered lots in Cape Coral in exchange for their parcels.

---

[33] quoted in Dodrill, *Selling the Dream*, p.57

[34] Rothchild, *Up for Grabs*, p.81

GAC Corporation eventually was declared bankrupt and reorganized as Avatar Holdings in 1980. The hotels were sold several times and housing developments have sprung up. There are plans for a 10-story apartment building. The Marina was bought by the County in 2009.

The legacy of Gulf American and GAC Properties is a warning. Vince Conboy, a vocal opponent, called it the "ditch it, dike it, drain it, sell fast and get out" mentality that led to the "largest land bust in the history of the world — a wilderness monster"[35]

### Writing in 1973, Archie Carr describes the tragedy:[36]

I had driven on out the Janes Road to where it was blocked by the outermost canal of a ghastly gridwork of ditches that real-estate developers have dug out there in the wilderness. I stopped at the new gash, sat on the excavated limestone bank, and watched the clear, dark water washing out westward toward the sea, racing away like blood out of a big cut artery.

### Skeet Johns said in an interview:[37]

They were digging a huge canal through the heart, actually separating the Picayune Strand from the Fakahatchee Strand and, in doing so, they destroyed the Picayune Strand. I mean, destroyed it. They made a totally different ecosystem. ... The amount of water that was being drained out of the swamp and simply going straight down the Fakaunion Canal into Chokoloskee Bay down there. It was 200,000 gallons of water a minute that was being drained out of the swamp. Consequently, with the Fakahatchee being a lower slough, it was able to survive but suffered a tremendous amount of damage itself. I would say, easily, 90 percent, if not 95 percent, of all the species of orchids died out because of lack of water in the swamp.

### Everglades City resident Foy Ballance commented:[38]

I saw lots of deer on Janes Drive before they dug the Remuda canal and built the Alley ... After the water was drained off that land, it messed up the whole country.

### In a 1976 article, Rick Gore wrote:[39]

They have created an environmental morass known as Golden Gate Estates. ... More than 140 miles of these canals undercut the Big Cypress watershed and pour off into the Gulf of Mexico almost 150 billion gallons of fresh water each year – enough to support a city of two million. "The Fakahatchee, I guarantee you, was the prettiest place in the state ten years ago," Collier County Deputy Sheriff Charlie Sanders told me angrily. "Now I can show you a grove where ghost orchids are shriveling up and falling off the trees, and bone-dry gator holes that a man had never seen the bottom of until they put those canals in."

---

[35] Conboy, *Esposé*, p.10

[36] Carr, *The Everglades*, p.52

[37] Michael Skeet Johns interview, 1999, online at University of Florida Digital Collection, George A. Smathers Library, SEM 251, pp 25-26

[38] quoted in Everglades City High School, *Prop Roots, Vol. III*, p.23

[39] Gore, Rick, "Twilight Hope for the Big Cypress", *National Geographic, vol. 150, no .2, August 1986*, p.262

Before Gulf American bought and developed the land, the logging company allowed locals to hunt. Ray Carroll remembers:[40]

> I grew up in Collier County and was first exposed to the Fakahatchee when my grandfathers put together a hunting club (the Six Club) in the late 1950s. They leased six or seven sections from Lee Tidewater Cypress, fenced it, built cabins, cooperated with Game & Fish Commission to manage the land, etc. I made several trips with them feeding the game, hunting, and just enjoying being in the woods. It was a wonderful experience for a young boy. The Club raised more turkey, deer & squirrels than I have seen since.

> The Six Club lease was two miles wide and it ran from half way up Dan House Prairie to just about where Janes Scenic Drive joins Stewart Boulevard. This was before Golden Gate Estates was developed; well before Alligator Alley was built, so I witnessed the last of the sheet flow trickle out of the Big Cypress Swamp. There was lots of water and it persisted so that the ground water table during the "dry" season was just below the surface of the ground. The prairies and woods were alive with frogs, crawfish, minnows and snails and that meant all the wildlife that fed on them too. It was really something to see.

Ralph Bellman describes walking westward from his hunting cabin in the Fakahatchee after Gulf American started developing:[41]

> The tree crusher ... would grab a tree and rip it up by the roots. All around this monster machine the land had been stripped of vegetation to the bare ground, leaving muck to bake in the sun. ... bird nests knocked to the ground, dead birds, hatchlings left to die, bucks, does crushed in the debris. Hundreds of dead animals ... wanton destruction ... by the mid-Seventies, Golden Gate Estates was bone dry. ... The Fakahatchee also felt the impact ... the water table there dropped about two feet, a dramatic change.

**The swamp buggy that Ray Carroll's grandfather had at the Six Club is seen here with Ray's friend Craig Neibauer on Fourstake Prairie where Ray & family have a camp on land acquired from previous GAC owners. *Photo courtesy of FOF member Ray Carroll.***

---

[40] email correspondence with the author

[41] quoted in Eastman, Susan, "Tales from the Swamp", *Miami Newtimes, July 31, 2003,* pp. 25-33

**Remuda Ranch (now called Port of the Islands).**
*Contemporary photos of the south hotel by the author.*
*Aerial photo taken in 1981 courtesy of Florida State Archives, Photographic Collection.*

The canals that drained away so much water in the "blocks" are being filled in.
*Top photo by the author, other photos courtesy of FOF member Dennis Giardina.*

# SAVING THE GREATER GLADES

To appreciate the environmental movement in South Florida, one has to look back almost a hundred years. In 1910, A. W. Dimock first wrote about his adventures in the glades in *Florida Enchantments* and advocated making the area into a National Park. He also suggested that hunters use cameras instead of guns!

Biologist Charles Torrey Simpson had visited south Florida from 1880 onwards and in 1920 expressed similar sentiments:[42]

> ... something very distressing in the gradual passing of the wilds, the destruction of the forests, the draining of the swamps and lowlands, the transforming of the prairies ... and in its place the coming of civilized man with his unsightly construction ... But I sometimes wonder quite seriously if the world is any better off because we have destroyed the wilds and filled the land with countless human beings.

In 1929 botanist John Kunkel Small warned about drainage in his book *From Eden to Sahara; Florida's Tragedy:*[43]

> Reckless, even wanton, devastation has now gained such headway that the future of North America's most prolific paradise seems to spell DESERT. This pecuniary greed ... is so great that few appear to be able or willing to see the handwriting on the map. Not only are Fauna and Flora threatened with extermination, but in many places the very soil which is necessary to their production and maintenance is being drained and burned and re-burned until nothing but inert mineral matter is left.

The Florida Federation of Women's Clubs had put pressure on the State and, with donations of land from the Flagler company, Paradise Key near Homestead was dedicated in 1916 as Royal Palm State Park. This was a first small step in recognizing that the Everglades were special.

Ernest F. Coe (a retired landscape architect) and John Pennekamp (editor of the *Miami Herald*) lobbied until Congress passed what was jokingly called the "Swamps and Alligators" act in 1934 that made provision for a future National Park in the area. The original boundaries included some 2 million acres, from Key Largo to north of the Tamiami Trail.

---

[42] Simpson, *In Lower Florida Wilds*, p.22

[43] Small, *From Eden to Sahara*, p.7

In 1934, forestry expert John Gifford wrote:[44]

> The purpose of this park will be educational, recreational and preservational, for all the people ... the wild life will be protected and many rare birds and other animals will be saved from extinction.

When President Harry S Truman read the dedication speech in Everglades City on December 6, 1947, Everglades National Park had been reduced in size because there were too many private landholders in the Big Cypress area, including the Collier company whose manager David Graham Copeland was chairman of the Park Boundary Commission.

The drainage continued. The Army Corps of Engineers riddled the remaining landscape with canals and dams. The land got drier and natural fires penetrated into the parched soil, killing potential seedlings. As John Kunkel Small had warned, parts of the greater glades were becoming a dust bowl.

National attention was finally drawn to the area in 1968 when Dade County proposed the Jetport, a huge international supersonic airport with massive runways and an extensive urban support system. The location — in the Big Cypress along the Tamiami Trail.

Conservationists got active and pointed out that changing the Big Cypress would starve the Everglades of even more water. The campaign was spearheaded by Marjory Stoneman Douglas whose book *The Everglades; River of Grass* in 1947 made her the "grandma of the glades". In 1971, President Nixon committed to saving the area and in 1974 the Big Cypress National Preserve was dedicated. The Jetport with one runway became a low-key training ground.

Closer to the Fakahatchee, there was concern about drainage when Corkscrew Swamp Sanctuary saw canals being dug at its doorstep by Gulf American. In 1965 the National Audubon Society raised funds, with help from the Ford Foundation, to purchase 2,640 acres as a buffer zone.

---

[44] Gifford, *On Preserving Tropical Florida*, p.96

# SAVING THE STRAND

Henry Ford and his pal Thomas Edison had winter homes in Fort Myers and made camping forays into the Big Cypress area to enjoy nature and collect plants. In 1922 Ford had an option from Turner and Burton to buy their land and offered to donate it to the State as a park. He was rejected because there were no public funds to maintain such an amenity. It was not until 1935 that Governor Scholtz signed legislation expanding the Board of Forestry into the Board of Forestry and Parks.

Long before Gulf American bought the land, concerned conservationist were worried about the future of this unique area. A report states that in 1948:[45]

> ... a nationally prominent citizens' group identified the Fakahatchee Strand as being worthy of public protection. The area was studied by the National Park Service and found to be unique and of national significance as a natural resource ... considered for acquisition as a State Park

and describes it:

> The Fakahatchee is particularly significant. This strand is a major slough draining the southwestern Big Cypress. Its mixture of cypress and royal palm is a rarity in forest types, and is considered among the most unusual and beautiful in the world.

Nothing much happened in the complacent 1950s as America's economy recovered from World War II during a politically conservative period. It was not until the early 1960s that Rachael Carson's *Silent Spring* was published. On a more local level, interest was focused on the Fakahatchee by a Miami lawyer named Mel Finn.

Melvin A. Finn, in an understated biographical sketch, gave his education as BA, MA, LLB (from Emory and the Universities of Georgia and Miami), his occupation as Attorney, and his interests as Conservation, Natural History, Writing, Nature Photography. These brief facts omit to say that he founded the Florida Nature Conservancy in 1961, classified 45 varieties of orchids in the Fakahatchee, and led the fight to save the strand from the early 1960s onward. Unfortunately, he did not survive heart surgery in November 1971 and never got to see the results of his campaigning.

---

[45] Everglades Jetport Advisory Board, *The Big Cypress Watershed,* Department of the Interior, Washington, DC, 1971, p.7

Franklin Adams recalls:[46]

Mel took many swamp walks, exploring and photographing orchids and wildlife. His enthusiasm was something to witness. Mel would get so excited when we spotted an orchid in bloom. More than once he tripped and fell into the water in his excitement. I remember telling him, "Mel, that orchid is not going anywhere, just calm down." I don't think he even heard me most of the time.

I first met Mel Finn when he called me. Someone had told him I had spent time in the swamp. My family had hunted in the Fak in the late 50s. We hit it off from the start and had some great times exploring the Fak. Like others who knew something about the area, we shared our knowledge eagerly with Mel. I eventually became a member of the Fakahatchee Strand Committee and wrote letters and accompanied Mel sometimes when he met with politicians.

In April 1962 the Fahkahatchee Strand Committee, a coalition of interested individuals, was formed at Mel's instigation. One of the activists was Mrs. Ben (Jane) Parks of Naples, Junior Conservation Chair of the Florida Federation of Women's Clubs, who collected petitions measuring 176 feet, gave talks, and rallied the media to the cause of making the Fakahatchee a State Park. Unfortunately, after the controversial "Alligator Alley" toll road was approved in September 1963, the J. C. Turner Lumber Company put up its price for the land to $100 per acre.

Even the weighty *New York Times* reported about the threats from drainage in neighboring Golden Gate Estates and the construction of the Alley. An article described the Fakahatchee as:[47]

South Florida's last available primeval watershed and true swamp area that functions as a self-sustaining ecological unit ... the existence of this sub-tropical wilderness may be threatened by progress – by the drainage of its water through newly constructed canals, by new roads, by bulldozers clearing land and by other manifestations of civilization.

Nixon Smiley wrote of his visit to the strand with Mel Finn:[48]

Despite the cutting of its forest of cypress less than a generation ago, despite the encroachment by hunters and greedy plant collectors, Fahkahatchee Strand holds it place as one of Florida's finest green jewels.

A move is now afoot by the Florida Nature Conservancy to preserve this sub-tropical swamp, so unusual that nothing like it exists anywhere else in North America.

---

[46] from notes for a speech loaned by Franklin Adams to the author

[47] Byram, John, "Florida Wilderness Area Imperiled", *The New York Times, September 27, 1964*

[48] Smiley, Nixon, "Can we Save our 'Green Jewel'?", *The Miami Herald, November 8, 1964*

The Department of the Interior was studying a proposal to make the Fakahatchee a National Monument while Mel Finn was also approaching the State.

In February 1966 Gulf American went ahead with the purchase of 68,000 acres from J. C. Turner and a spokesman is quoted as saying "present plans are to fence the tract and stock it with deer, wild hogs and wild turkey."[49]

In February 1966 Franklin Adams wrote to Congressman Paul Rogers in Washington, DC:[50]

> We have all known this county as the "Last Frontier", but due to increased real estate development the frontier has passed from Collier County and so has much of its natural beauty.
>
> It is now time for those who feel a responsibility for the county's future to be vigilant to preserve and protect some of the unique natural settings which have attracted so many permanent as well as seasonal visitors to it.
>
> The area of which I am concerned is the Fakahatchee Strand of Collier County. The hour is late and direct action must be taken to save this truly unique ecological area. For it is certainly worth much more as one of nature's masterpieces than as just another tract of land to be exploited for the temporary monetary gain of a few individuals.
>
> Areas such as this can and should belong to all the people, and remain to provide a place for relaxation and renewal of one's self away from the fast pace of our daily lives.
>
> I would therefore ask you to devote your full support to having Fakahatchee Strand preserved as a National Monument.

A bill to save the Fakahatchee was introduced by Congressman Rogers in March. Unfortunately for the Fakahatchee, the federal budget was spent to create Biscayne National Monument, another pressing cause. Gulf American began to market Remuda Ranch Grants and to develop the two hotels adjacent to the Trail near the Faka Union Canal.

A Federal Water Quality report in late 1969 recommended that drainage be stopped in the adjacent "blocks" and Mel Finn wrote to the Collier County Commissioners. For economic as well as environmental reasons, GAC ceased dredging and selling lots early in 1970. The company even offered to sell 20,000 acres to the State (at $125 per acre, only $25 above their original purchase price).

---

[49] quoted in "Gulf American Buys Big Tract At Fakahatchee", *Collier County News, February 11, 1966*

[50] from a copy of the letter loaned by Franklin Adams to the author

Franklin Adams describes a turning point in negotiations with the State:[51]

On April 30th, 1970, Mel and I travelled to Everglades City in order to take a group into the Fak the next morning on May 1st. Among that group was Nat Reed (Governor Claude Kirk's conservation advisor), Joel Kuperberg (director of Caribbean Gardens in Naples and co-founder of the Collier County Conservancy), Ney Landrum (director of what became Florida State Parks), Ken Alvarez (a new biologist at Florida Division of Recreation & Parks), and George Gardner (Special Assistant for the Environment for the State).

Mel did a slide show at the Rod & Gun Club where all of them stayed the night. Mel and I shared a room at the cheaper "Illinois Motel" which is known today as the Everglades Motel. During the night I received a call that my mother had passed away in Miami so I returned home immediately.

Mel and the group went into the Fak that morning. That visit really impressed Nat Reed and the others. They gave their full support to trying to acquire the Fak.

Biologist F. C. Craighead in 1971 wrote "the Fahkahatchee Strand or Slough ... is one of the prized features of the Big Cypress"[52]

As a postscript to a lavishly-illustrated article about the Fakahatchee by Mel Finn in their company magazine, GAC wrote:[53]

The property was purchased in 1966 from the J. C. Turner Lumber Company and for three years was offered for public sale as recreational land. From the outset, it was made clear to buyers that the Strand would never be drained and that no construction could take place there. ... the company had the wisdom to withhold from sale the drainage easements in Fahkahatchee. Now, all of GAC's remaining acreage in the Strand, including these drainage reserves, have been offered to the state for about half the appraised value ... GAC Corporation does care about preserving this priceless wildlife area for generations to come. ... We hope the company's efforts to safeguard this area by conveying it into public ownership will arrest this particular threat to our vanishing wilderness area.

This does not quite agree with the interview given by Charles Hepner, an advertising man who had worked with the Rosen brothers since their Baltimore days:[54]

The tragedy really was Remuda ... We were going to drain that. Then we were going to let a stream back in and then we became the bad guys because they didn't let us do it. ... We put in that main building a big restaurant, all that sea wall in there and all those docks in there. We put an airstrip in there. We put in the tennis courts and the big pool. It was a gorgeous building. ... We put in all kind of amenities there, and then we were told you can't drain the land.

---

[51] from notes for a speech loaned by Franklin Adams to the author

[52] reproduced in McCluney, *The Environmental Destruction of South Florida*, p.11

[53] *The GAC Magazine, Spring 1971,* GAC Corporation, Miami, FL, p.66

[54] *Interview with Charles Hepner,* January 3, 1988, Samuel Proctor Oral History Program, University of Florida Digital Collections, pp. 29-30

In 1972 a referendum was passed authorizing the State to issue bonds totaling $240 million to buy Environmentally Endangered Lands. In May of 1973, GAC gave the State 9,523 acres south of the Trail in compensation for over-dredging at Cape Coral by Gulf American some ten years previously. The Collier County Conservancy donated another 2,000 acres.

Finally, in March 1974 the Florida Department of Natural Resources proposed to the cabinet that the State buy 24,568 acres from GAC for $4.4 million ($179 per acre) plus whatever parcels were returned to the company by private landowners. Governor Reubin Askew is quoted as saying "protection of the Fakahatchee Strand should receive high priority."[55] The cabinet approved the purchase.

In 1975, a further 357 acres was given to the State by GAC for over-dredging and in December 1976 the State bought 8,761 acres from GAC at $382 per acre.

In 1975 the State asked the Collier County Commissioners to donate the three sections they owned in the middle of the Fakahatchee. The land had been given to the County by Gulf American as part of their development bond during the Remuda years so that it could be made into a park. In 1982 the County signed a long-term lease with the State for the 1,920 acres. However, one of the Commissioners wanted a mineral study done in case there was oil under the ground.

In 1977, hunting and vehicles were prohibited in parts of the Strand. In 1982 a request to close the north end of Janes Scenic Drive was denied by the County Commissioners. The State worried that it could not control poaching. Eventually, the County handed over the road to the State in September 2004.

The purchases of land in the Fakahatchee continues as original Remuda owners decide to sell their lots.

On April 24, 1999, a memorial to Mel Finn was dedicated in front of the Park headquarters in Copeland. A large hunk of limestone was selected by Park manager Greg Toppin from the neighboring Harmon Brothers

---

[55] "GAC Land", *Naples Daily News, 3/29/1974*

Rockpit to hold the bronze plaque which commemorates the "Father of the Fahkahatchee". Among those present at the unveiling were Fran Mainella (Director of the Florida DEP Division of Recreation and Parks), Ney Landrum (past director of the Division), Joel Kuperberg, and Nathaniel Reed plus many well-wishers.

---

"FATHER OF THE FAHKAHATCHEE"

Mel Finn

1916 - 1971

Georgia native, adopted son of Florida, U. S. Army Air Corps veteran, U. of Miami graduate, attorney, founder of the Florida Nature Conservancy, member of Tropical Audubon, South Florida Orchid Society and self-trained field biologist, he criss-crossed the cutover Fahkahatchee, identified 45 varieties of orchids, nine found nowhere else.

Mel was the Fahkahatchee's voice, dogged, persistent, abrasive, whatever it took; he badgered nature groups, led chest-deep field trips, wrote appeals to preserve this once mightiest of South Florida cypress strands. An ailing heart took him before his dream was realized but he had made his point. Florida funded acquisition, a buy-back program still underway.

Today, because of Mel Finn's vision and persistence, you enjoy the recovering Fahkahatchee, main artery in the circulatory system of Southwest Florida. Outgrowth of Mel's dream, a wilderness greenway now stretches fifty miles from the southeast corner of Lee County to the waters of Florida Bay. Gulf of Mexico Greenway links are Corkscrew Regional Ecosystem Watershed, Florida Panther National Wildlife Refuge, Fahkahatchee State Preserve and the Ten-Thousand Island National Wildlife Refuge.

Mel, you made believers out of the rest of us and

were a pioneer in Florida's land conservation efforts.

*Friends of Mel Finn - 1998*

---

Unveiling the Mel Finn monument in front of the office in Copeland on April 24, 1999.
*Photo from the Friends of Fakahatchee scrapbook.*

Mel Finn in the Fakahatchee. There was a drought in 1971.
*Photos courtesy of FOF member Franklin Adams.*

Weaver's Camp station at Big Cypress Bend. Note the water barrel near the sheds.
*Sketch from the 1973 Collier County 50th Anniversary commemorative calendar.*

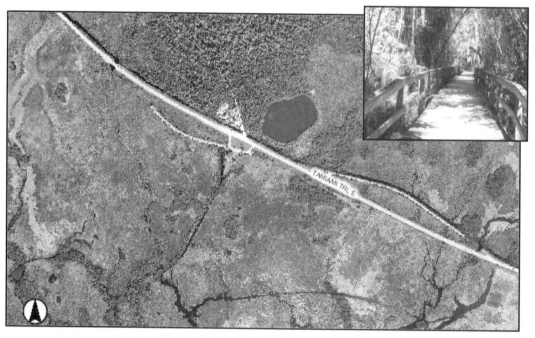

**Big Cypress Bend: Weaver's Camp site on south, Indian village and Boardwalk on north.**
*Aerial photo courtesy of the Collier County Property Appraiser.*
*Inset photo of boardwalk by the author.*

# BIG CYPRESS BEND

After the Tamiami Trail was completed in 1928, six stations were built to service motorists along the unpaved road. Patrolmen on motorcycles travelled up and down the Trail, looking for stranded vehicles. Gasoline and snacks were available for sale at the stations, which were owned by the Collier company. They were described as "a country general store with a gas pump."[56]

The Fakahatchee Station, near the head of the river, was also known as Weaver's Camp after its operator who kept it open after the patrol was dissolved in 1934. Besides the main building, there were cabins where people could stay overnight. The Indian village was established as early as 1938 by Robert and Suzie Billie who sold crafts to tourists.

The area is officially referred to as Big Cypress Bend.

After hearing that the virgin cypress would be logged, conservationist and philanthropist Lester Norris of Keewaydin in Naples bought the section (some 600 acres) and built a boardwalk. He also bought Weaver's Camp which Joe Simmons operated and offered airboat rides in the 1970s.

In 1966, it was named a National Natural Landmark by the National Park Service who describe it as:[57]

> Big Cypress Bend includes undisturbed virgin cypress, sawgrass prairie, and palmetto hammocks ... the site is probably the best sizeable example of a tropical swamp remaining in the Southeast. It contains the largest royal palm stand in the country.

In 1976 the State bought the tract, except for the station, and in 1977 Lester Norris donated funds to repair the Boardwalk. He is quoted as saying:[58]

> ... the money designated for the Big Cypress Bend boardwalk will make accessible to the public acres of rare floral plants and stands of cypress trees estimated by conservationists to be over 700 years old. We wanted to keep it for posterity. We are happy to know that the state finally bought it.

---

[56] Jacobs, James A., *Historic American Buildings Survey; Monroe Station,* HABS No. FL-544, Washington, DC, p.26

[57] from website www.nature.nps.gov/nnl

[58] quoted in Herendeen, Steve, "Norris Family Donates Money to Help Parks", *Naples Daily News, January 24, 1977,* p.1

The 10-acre Weaver's Camp parcel was finally sold several times and is now owned by the Miccosukee Tribe. All but a couple of dilapidated sheds remain after the main building was demolished and the cypress water barrels were removed.

The Trail was straightened and widened in 1995. Remnants of the old road are visible to the north and south of US-41.

The Boardwalk is a popular tourist attraction during the winter season, allowing visitors from all over the world to get a glimpse of the Fakahatchee without getting their feet wet. Volunteers from the Friends of Fakahatchee often welcome tourists and answer their questions. One highlight is the Bald Eagles' nest which usually has chicks in January. Another popular spot is the alligator pond at the end of the 2500-foot elevated walk.

An eco-friendly visitors' center and improvements to the Boardwalk are being considered by the Friends and the Park.

**Volunteers from the Friends of Fakahatchee greet visitors to the Boardwalk.**
*Photo courtesy of FOF members Caryl & Nelson Tilden.*

# THE PRESERVE AND FRIENDS

The Fakahatchee Strand Preserve State Park is now some 80,000 acres. Although it was declared a "Park" by the Florida Park Service to standardize all the State's holdings, it is essentially a Preserve. The public can gain access on the unpaved Janes Memorial Scenic Drive but are warned not to stray off the side trams. Tens of thousands of visitors each year get an impression of the Fakahatchee when they take a gentle stroll on the Boardwalk at Big Cypress Bend.

There are still some private landholders within the Preserve, a few of whom have established camps while others are absentee owners and may not even be aware that they have inherited the parcel.

The Fakahatchee and its rare Ghost Orchid came to national notice when *New Yorker* magazine journalist Susan Orlean wrote the book *The Orchid Thief* which was made into a film in 2002 called "Adaption", starring Nicolas Cage and Meryl Streep. The preview in Naples on December 19, 2002, attracted people who wanted to learn more about the drama at their back doorsteps.

By that time the Friends of Fakahatchee (FOF) had been formed. The mission of this "Citizen Support Organization" is to preserve the Fakahatchee and to teach the public about it. The group works closely with the Park manager, volunteering time for special projects and contributing funds. As a 501(c)(3) not-for-profit corporation, FOF is in a position to accept donations from individuals and companies.

The Friends got together in late 1997 at the instigation of former Park manager Greg Toppin and Park biologist Mike Owen. Their first meeting was held in the Copeland Baptist Mission (now Church). Some of those early members are still involved. The official incorporation was filed by the State of Florida on May 4, 1998, with a covering letter from the director of the Parks Division certifying that the Friends of Fakahatchee Strand State Preserve, Inc., is authorized to provide support for the Park.

FOF had a membership in 2009 of more than 250 people on both the east and west coasts of Florida as well as in other states and even in

Switzerland and England. It issues periodic newsletters, maintains a website, and conducts guided swamp walks and canoe tours. Members participate in work days to help the park, greet visitors at the boardwalk, give educational talks, attend festivals to distribute their literature, and enjoy social events.

When the FOF Directors feel that it is deserved, they give the Mel Finn Award to an individual who has contributed to the Fakahatchee. The special plaque reads:

FRIENDS OF FAKAHATCHEE STRAND STATE PRESERVE
MEL FINN AWARD
FOR REFLECTING THE SPIRIT OF THE FOUNDING FATHERS OF THE FSSP

Recipients thus far are Elsa Caldwell, Barbara Lewinski, Don Harmon, Dennis Marlin, Franklin Adams, John Elting, Allen Caldwell, and Nelson Tilden.

The Park is well-known in the Southwest District of the DEP Parks Division for its active CSO and for its unique ecology. One never knows what one will see!

In 2004, the rare "Mossy Helmet" orchid *(Cranichis muscosa)*, last observed in the early 1900s, was spotted by part-time biological assistant Karen Relish and reported by volunteer Russ Clusman in the FOF newsletter:[59]

> Karen, while slogging, was intently recording the rare flora she encountered up in the tree branches, cypress knees, stumps and logs (fallen dead trees). Something different caught her eye so she called out to Mike [Owen, Park biologist] for further examination. There on a seven-foot long prostrate log laden with moss was a group of small plants with their roots embedded in the abundant moss. Several plants were in bloom ...

Florida panthers and black bears are more common sights although still rare. The Everglades mink is also present. There is a wealth of orchids, bromeliads, and ferns that are not seen elsewhere.

A Level 1 Archeological Survey in 2007 documented over 80 sites, many of them the ruins of hunting camps (tumbled-down shacks, old stoves,

---

[59] Clusman, Russell, "Lost for a Century", *The Ghost Writer, May 2004,* Friends of Fakahatchee, special insert. See www.friendsoffakahatchee.org

broken crockery) or abandoned vehicles but a few possibly pre-historic middens with bones and pottery shards. The authors of the survey recommended that the system of trams be considered for inclusion on the National Register of Historic Places as being characteristic of logging practices before conservation was considered. Also mentioned is that the raised tram beds allowed hunters and hikers to explore what had been an almost impenetrable area.

Preservation and maintenance are the goals of those who love the Fakahatchee. Tom Maish, FOF President in 2009, said he joined because:[60]

> The uniqueness of the Fakahatchee and other parts of the south Florida eco-system must be preserved for our children's children to enjoy and also appreciate. That is why I love to work for and in the Fakahatchee.

He is not the only one who has caught the "Fak-a-Habit", a term coined by Bill Mesce who leads swamp walks for the Friends and lives on the fringes of the Preserve. The catch phrase was used by photographer and FOF member Jay Staton as the title of his hour-long DVD which has spectacular pictures of native plants and animals accompanied by natural sounds.

Another volunteer, Jean Stefanik from New Hampshire who wrote the initial Level 1 archaeological survey grant application in collaboration with staff and other FOF volunteers, said:[61]

> I love the wilderness aspect of Fakahatchee, and the ability to discover new plants and animals literally every time visiting. I love the camaraderie, the quality and motivations of the people involved with the Friends, and the spirit of service in preserving and gently and thoughtfully developing (or not) this wild area.

Patty Huff, FOF president 2003-2004, remembers early days when the group met quarterly and there would be cookies home-made by secretary Kerrie Chobot who "held the group together". She recalls:[62]

> We would hold annual picnics in the Fakahatchee. It was very informal but attracted many members. Greg would do a cook-out and everyone would bring a side dish. Cindy Hackney would play her guitar. Mike Owen would take us on swamp walks.

---

[60] email correspondence with the author

[61] email correspondence with the author

[62] email correspondence with the author

Pam Mesce, another founding member, said the they were "fun days"[63] and Barbara Lewinski, former FOF officer, said that they helped with exotic removal and had weekend meetings in a friend's hunting cabin. She also enjoyed helping with the annual Slough Survey conducted by Park biologist Mike Owen.

Former Park manager Greg Toppin sums it up:[64]

When I came to Fakahatchee there was the remnants of a CSO that was combined with Collier-Seminole. The treasurer was the only one left that had anything to do with Fakahatchee. I decided to re-start the CSO at Fakahatchee as a standalone, on its own feet so to speak, in order to specifically benefit Fakahatchee. The early days were short on numbers of people participating, but it was fun. We actually held work days, did canoe trips and swamp walks, and held a couple of picnics. We also had booths at the fair, seafood festival, Big Cypress Anniversary, and sent representatives to the annual volunteer meeting. Volunteers worked on projects such as swamp buggies, data recording, administrative duties, and publicity. We would meet in the office at the park. Briefly, this was the beginning. But I think most importantly it was fun and the Fakahatchee is better for it.

**Friends of Fakahatchee picnic in March 1998.**
**Park manager Greg Toppin in center and Cindy Hackney singing on the buggy.**
*Photo from the Friends of Fakahatchee scrapbook.*

---

[63] interview with the author, 10/14/09

[64] email correspondence with the author

Hurricane Wilma struck the Fakahatchee in October 2005. Park staff and volunteers cleaned up the Boardwalk (left) within a month. Jones Grade was tackled by some of the Friends.
*Photos courtesy of FOF members Dennis Giardina and Jim & Niki Woodard.*

Guided Swamp Walks are organized by the Friends during the winter season.
*Photo courtesy of FOF member Mitch Mitchell.*

The Friends' booth at the Miami International Orchid Show in 2004.
*Photo courtesy of FOF members Jim & Niki Woodard.*

Board of Directors and Members at the FOF annual meeting in April 2008.
*Photo by the author.*

# SOURCES

Tebeau's *Man in the Everglades* is a good place to start for a history of this part of south Florida from the earliest days until the late 1960s. His *Florida's Last Frontier* deals more specifically with the settlement of Collier County and the building of the Tamiami Trail.

Grunwald's *The Swamp* is profusely annotated with references about drainage and reclamation.

For the logging industry, Kendrick's *History of Florida Forests* is the classic and the 2007 edition with notes by Barry Walsh brings it up to date.

Doderill's *Selling the Dream* about Gulf American and GAC Properties provides the background to the Golden Gate Estates and Remuda Ranch Grants developments while Carter's *The Florida Experience* and Conboy's *Exposé* provide the criticism.

The Internet gives researchers a wealth of information at their fingertips. Many of the pictures in this book came from the Florida State Archives Photographic Collection (www.floridamemory.com) and some of the background documents were read on www.palmm.fcla.edu, which links to Florida academic and museum collections. The useful www.books.google.com and www.archive.org are online libraries where one can read older books and sample newer ones.

The Collier County Public Library and the Inter-Library Loan system deliver books and bound reports which can be requested via their websites.

For information about the Park and the Friends, see:

www.floridastateparks.org/fakahatcheestrand

www.friendsoffakahatchee.org

Abbey, Kathryn Trimmer, **Florida, Land of Change**, 1941: University of North Carolina Press, Chapel Hill, NC. *(general history, politics)*

Alderson, Doug, **The Ghost Orchid Ghost and Other Tales from the Swamp**, 2007: Pineapple Press, Sarasota, FL. *(ghost stories, one set in the Fakahatchee)*

Allan, Leslie, Beryle Kuder and Sara L. Oakes, **Promised Lands, Volume 2: Subdivisions in Florida's Wetlands**, 1977: Inform, Inc, New York, NY. *(survey of 9 developments)*

Barbour, Thomas, **That Vanishing Eden; A Naturalist's Florida**, 1944: Little, Brown and Company, Boston, MA. *(travels, against drainage/development)*

Becerra, Cesar A., **Giants of the Swamp; The Story of South Florida's Logging Industry**, 1994: www.planetcesar.com, Miami, FL. *(report, clippings, interviews, mostly about the Jones Lumber Company, prepared for a traveling exhibit)*

Brown, Loren G., **Totch; A Life in the Everglades**, 1993: University Press of Florida, Gainesville, FL. *(biography about living in the Ten Thousand Islands, fishing & hunting, smuggling)*

Burghard, August, **Alligator Alley; Florida's Most Controversial Highway**, 1969: Lanman Company, Washington, DC. *(history of road, travel guide along the way)*

Carr, Archie, **The Everglades**, 1973: Time-Life Books, New York, NY. *(color photos, lyrical descriptions)*

Carter, Luther J., **The Florida Experience; Land and Water Policy in a Growth State**, 1974: Johns Hopkins University Press, Baltimore, MD. *(drainage, development, politics, parks)*

Carter, W. Hodding, **Stolen Water; Saving the Everglades from Its Friends, Foes, and Florida**, 2004: Atria Books, New York, NY. *(cynical look at drainage and restoration)*

Cerulean, Susan, ed., **The Book of the Everglades**, 2002: Milkweed Editions, Minneapolis, MN. *(articles from noted contributors)*

Conboy, Vince, **Exposé; Florida's Billion Dollar Land Fraud**, n/d: printed privately. *(criticism of Gulf American development)*

Craighead, Sr., Frank C., **The Trees of South Florida, Volume I; The Natural Environments and Their Succession**, 1971: University of Miami Press, Coral Gables, FL. *(drainage, environment)*

Davis, Jr, John H., "The Natural Features of Southern Florida, Especially the Vegetation, and the Everglades", 1943: *Florida Geological Survey, Bulletin 25*, Tallahassee, FL. *(survey of the area by ecologist, history)*

Dimock, A. W., **Florida Enchantments**, 1915: A. W. Dimock, Peekamose, NY. *(chapters about trips in the Glades)*

Dodrill, David E., **Selling the Dream; The Gulf American Corporation and the Building of Cape Coral, Florida**, 1993: University of Alabama Press, Tuscaloosa, AL. *(Rosen brothers, includes Remuda Ranch and Golden Gate Estates)*

Douglas, Marjory Stoneman, **The Everglades; River of Grass**, 1947: reprinted in 1974 by Mockingbird, Marietta, GA. *(history of Glades, plea for conservation)*

Dovell, J. E., "The Everglades Before Reclamation", 1947: *Florida Historical Quarterly, vol. 26, no. 1*, FHS, St Augustine, FL. *(anthropology, Seminole Wars, drainage)*

Dovell, J. E., "Thomas Elmer Will, Twentieth Century Pioneer", 1948: *Tequesta, No. VIII*, HMSF, Miami, FL. *(drainage, land sales, farming near Lake)*

Duever, Michael J., et. al., **The Big Cypress National Preserve,** 1986: National Audubon Society, New York, NY. (reprint of 1979 report to Dept of Interior)

Everglades City High School, **Prop Roots, Vol. II; Hermits from the Mangrove Country of the Everglades**, n/d: Collier County Public Schools, Everglades City, FL. *(local interviews)*

Everglades City High School, **Prop Roots, Vol. III; Hunting Stories from the Mangrove Country of the Everglades**, 1984: Collier County Public Schools, Everglades City, FL. *(local interviews)*

Ewel, Katherine Carter, and Howard T. Odlum, eds, **Cypress Swamps**, 1984: University Presses of Florida, Gainesville, FL. *(collection of research papers)*

Fritchey, John (ed. Beth R. Read), **Everglades Journal**, 1992: Florida Heritage Press, Miami, FL. *(biography, life in the swamps, environment)*

Gifford, John C., **The Everglades and Other Essays Relating to Southern Florida**, 1911: Everglade Land Sales Co., Miami, FL. *(reprints of articles, tribute to Broward)*

Gifford, John C., **The Reclamation of the Everglades with Trees**, 1935: Books Inc., New York, NY. *(suggested plants for drainage)*

Gifford, John C. with Elizabeth Ogren Rothra, **On Preserving Tropical Florida**, 1972: University of Miami Press, Miami, FL. *(biographical notes, reprints of articles)*

Grunwald, Michael, **The Swamp; The Everglades, Florida, and the Politics of Paradise**, 2006: Simon & Schuster, New York, NY. *(history of drainage and restoration, Army Corps of Engineers)*

Hammond, James, **Florida's Vanishing Trail**, 2008: www.lulu.com, *(Indian forts, towns along Tamiami Trail)*

Harrington, Drew, "Burton-Swartz Cypress Company of Florida", 1985: *Florida Historical Quarterly, vol. 63, no. 4*, FHS, St Augustine, FL. *(activity in Perry)*

Henshall, James A., M.D., **Camping and Cruising in Florida**, 1884: Robert Clarke & Co, Cincinnati, OH. *(travels, Seminoles)*

Hrdlicka, Ales, *The Anthropology of Florida*, 1922: Florida State Historical Society, Deland, FL. *(description of archeological survey)*

Kendrick, Baynard, and Barry Walsh, **A History of Florida Forests**, 2007: University Press of Florida, Gainesville, FL. *(comprehensive history from Kendrick's 1967 draft, updated and annotated by Walsh)*

La Plante, Leah, "The Sage of Biscayne Bay; Charles Torrey Simpson's Love Affair with South Florida", 1995: *Tequesta, No. LX*, HMSF, Miami, FL. *(biography with quotations)*

Larson, Ron, **Swamp Song; A Natural History of Florida's Swamps**, 1995: University Press of Florida, Gainesville, FL. *(background, flora & fauna, visits)*

Levin, Ted, "A Singular Swamp; Florida's Fakahatchee Strand is too wild to be wholly known - or even surveyed", *Audubon magazine, July-August 1994*, National Audubon Society, New York, NY. *(contemporary visit)*

Levin, Ted, **Liquid Land: A Journey through the Florida Everglades**, 2003: University of Georgia Press, Athens, GA. *(ecology, restoration, references)*

Luer, Carlyle A., **The Native Orchids of Florida**, 1972: New York Botanical Garden, New York, NY. *(large illustrated reference)*

McCally, David, **The Everglades, An Environmental History**, 1999: University Press of Florida, Gainesville, FL. *(origins, drainage, development)*

McCluney, William Ross, ed., **The Environmental Destruction of South Florida; A Handbook for Citizens**, 1971: University of Miami Press, Coral Gables, FL. *(collection of articles by Craighead, Marshall, Browder, etc)*

McIver, Stuart, **Dreamers, Schemers, and Scalawags**, 1994: Pineapple Press, Sarasota, FL. *(Florida Chronicles, historical articles)*

McIver, Stuart, **True Tales of the Everglades**, 1989: Florida Flair Books, Miami, FL. *(short articles about historic subjects)*

Mullins, Sr., L. D., **As I Remember**, 1966: printed privately. *(memoirs of farmer and sawmill owner, cut Collier pine near Bonita Springs)*

O'Reilly, John, "South Florida's Amazing Everglades", *National Geographic, January, 1940*, Washington, DC. *(trip with Audubon wardens, mostly birding)*

Orlean, Susan, **The Orchid Thief**, 1998: Random House, New York, NY. *(by New Yorker columnist, about stealing ghost orchids in the Fak, made into movie "Adaptation")*

Peterman, Frank & Audrey, **African Americans and the Sawmills of Big Cypress; A Brief History**, n/d, National Park Service, Ochopee, FL. *(report, interviews with local people, probably 2002)*

Rothchild, John, **Up for Grabs**, 1985: University Press of Florida, Gainesville, FL. *(personal story, lived in Everglades City in 1970s, criticism of Golden Gate Estates development)*

Simpson, Charles Torrey, **In Lower Florida Wilds**, 1920: G. P. Putnam's Sons, New York and London. *(botanist's observations)*

Small, John Kunkel, **From Eden to Sahara, Florida's Tragedy**, 1929: The Science Press Printing Company, Lancaster, PA. *(warning about drainage)*

Smiley, Nixon, **Florida, Land of Images**, 1977: E. A. Seemann Publishing, Inc, Miami, FL. *(articles about Florida, biographical notes)*

Smiley, Nixon, **On the Beat and Offbeat**, 1983: Banyan Books, Miami, FL. *(Miami Herald articles by respected journalist)*

Sprunt, Jr., Alexander, "Emerald Kingdom", *Audubon magazine, January 1961*, New York, NY. *(article about Corkscrew acquisition, environment)*

Stone, C. R., **Forty Years in the Everglades**, 1979: Atlantic Publishing Co., Tabor City, NC. *(memories of hunter/explorer from 1930s)*

Stone, Maria, **Caxambas Kid; The Life & Times of the Famous Fishing Guide Preston Sawyer**, 1987: Butterfly Press, Naples, FL. *(biography of Marco fisherman)*

Stone, Maria, **We Also Came; Black People of Collier County**, 1992: Butterfly Press, Naples, FL. *(interviews with local people, some involved in logging)*

Storter, Rob, **Crackers in the Glade; Life and Times in the Old Everglades**, 2000: University of Georgia Press, Athens, GA. *(stories and sketches about his life)*

Swain, Randolph, **Memories of Randolph Swain**, 1989: P K Younge Library of Florida History, Gainesville, FL. *(superintendent of Lee Tidewater Cypress in Copeland)*

Tebeau, Charlton W., **Florida's Last Frontier; The History of Collier County**, 1966: University of Miami Press, Coral Gables, FL. *(classic history of the area)*

Tebeau, Charlton W., **Man in the Everglades; 2000 Years of Human History in the Everglades National Park**, 1968: University of Miami Press, Coral Gables, FL. *(from early Indians to Park)*

Turner, Gregg M., **Railroads of Southwest Florida**, 1999: Arcadia Publishing, Charleston, SC. *(history with many old photos)*

Willoughby, Hugh L., **Across the Everglades; A Canoe Journey of Exploration**, 1913: J. B. Lippincott Company, Philadelphia, PA. *(early travels)*

# TIMELINE

| | |
|---|---|
| 1845 | Florida made the 27th State in the USA |
| 1858 | Third Seminole War ended |
| 1870 | white settlers arrived in SW Florida |
| 1881 | Disston started draining Kissimmee area |
| 1887 | Lee County established (included Fakahatchee) |
| 1896 | railroad arrived in Miami |
| 1904 | railroad arrived in Fort Myers |
| **1913** | **J.C. Turner & Capt. Burton bought land in Fakahatchee** |
| 1916 | Royal Palm State Park dedicated near Homestead |
| **1922** | **Henry Ford offered to buy Fakahatchee for the State** |
| **1924** | **Lee Cypress Company incorporated** |
| 1923 | Barron Collier bought land, Collier County established (included Fakahatchee) |
| 1927 | Florida Board of Forestry established |
| 1928 | Tamiami Trail, Immokalee Road, and ACL railroad to Everglades town completed |
| 1935 | Florida Park Service established under Forestry Board |
| **1943** | **Lee Tidewater Cypress Company started logging in the area** |
| 1947 | Everglades National Park dedicated, "Everglades, River of Grass" published |
| **1947** | **Lee Cypress Company name changed to Lee Tidewater Cypress** |
| 1956 | Corkscrew Sanctuary established by Audubon Society |
| **1957** | **Lee Tidewater Cypress Company stopped logging in the area** |
| 1960 | Gulf American started buying land for Golden Gate Estates |
| **1961** | **Mel Finn founded Florida chapter of Nature Conservancy** |
| **1966** | **Gulf American bought Fakahatchee, started Remuda Ranch Grants** |
| 1968 | Jetport started in Big Cypress |
| 1972 | Environmentally Endangered Lands act passed by State |
| **1974** | **Fakahatchee declared a State Preserve** |
| 1974 | Big Cypress National Preserve dedicated |
| **1976** | **Fakahatchee boardwalk area (Norris Tract) sold to the State** |
| 1989 | Florida Panther NWR established |
| 1991 | Picayune acquired as a State Forest |
| 1996 | Ten Thousand Islands NWR established |
| **1997** | **Friends of Fakahatchee first met** |
| **2000** | **Fakahatchee declared a State "Park"** |
| 2000 | Comprehensive Everglades Restoration Plan approved |